D1624015

Stake Your Claim

EMMET FOX

Stake Your Claim

HARPER & ROW, PUBLISHERS
New York, Hagerstown, San Francisco, London

Contents

5

CONTENTS

CONTENTS

CONTENTS

Foreword

FOR MORE THAN TWENTY YEARS I HAVE BEEN CLOSELY associated with Dr. Emmet Fox, as assistant, companion, and friend. During those twenty years Dr. Fox has probably influenced the lives of more people than any other single individual. One of his booklets alone, "The Golden Key," has sold over a half million copies, and hundreds of thousands of people have heard his lectures from coast to coast.

The essays in this book I consider the refined gold of his lifetime of teaching and helping people. They have been written in an easy-to-read-and-understand style. Each one is a time-tested recipe for accomplishment and well-being. You can have true success and happiness in life if you will consistently put these truths into practice in your daily living.

It is your God-given duty to Stake Your Claim to peace, poise, power, prosperity, and health—and God expects you to be satisfied with nothing less.

HERMAN WOLHORN

Stake Your Claim

Now I Speak the Word*

GOD IS INFINITE LIFE. GOD IS BOUNDLESS LOVE. GOD is Infinite Intelligence. God is Unfathomable Wisdom. God is Unspeakable Beauty. God is the Unchanging Principle of Perfect Good. God is the Soul of man.

I am the image and likeness of God, and I have the power of the Word. When I speak that Word, it goes forth and cannot return void. It accomplishes the thing whereunto I send it. That Word goes forth charged with the power of God.

Now I speak the Word in your name and in mine. I invoke the power of the Healing Christ, and I say that the full power of God is now awakened in you, filling your soul with peace and life and joy. God is Light, and that Light fills your Soul. Your Soul is as the burning bush that burned with the power of God and was not

* This meditation, and others very similar to it, were used by Dr. Fox at many of the Sunday morning services which he conducted in such well-known places as the Biltmore and Astor Hotels, the old Hippodrome, the Manhattan Opera House, and in Carnegie Hall.

It forms a powerful prayer and can be used in whole or in part as a daily meditation.—H.W.

consumed. There are no dark corners left; no complexes or neuroses; no fears or doubts; no old dark things. God is Light and in Him there is no darkness at all. God is Life and that Life builds every cell in your body. The tide of Divine Life sweeps through your body, carrying before It any toxins, any foreign things that should not be there. It reforms, re-creates, regenerates every organ and tissue, and charges it with Its own Divine Life.

I claim that the peace of God surrounds you and fills you. That peace goes with you as a pillar of cloud by day and a pillar of fire by night. In that peace, and that health, and that harmony you dwell.

I claim that the power of God goes before you and makes your path straight. It opens your way for true prosperity, for freedom, for unlimited spiritual growth.

I claim that God will bring into your life the right people who can help you and make you happy, and that those whom you do not wish will fade out of your existence and prosper elsewhere.

I claim that all that God is, is now working to move you into your true place. The outer thing is but a picture, and the power of God is changing your picture now and moving you into your true place.

One Presence, one Power, and one Mind. One God,

one Law, one Element. You are part of that Divine Presence and in that Presence you dwell forever. . . .

And according to your faith it shall be done unto you.

☙

Putting Isaac on the Wood Pile

And God said, take now thy son, thine only son Isaac, whom thou lovest, and get thee into the land of Moriah; and offer him there for a burnt-offering upon one of the mountains which I will tell thee of. GENESIS 22:2

EVERYONE KNOWS THE STORY OF THE TEMPTATION of Abraham. The important point is to realize that it is not just an incident that happened thousands of years ago, but that it happens to everyone on the spiritual path in all ages right down to the present day.

Abraham was required to sacrifice the thing that he loved best on earth, his only son, the child that had come to him by a miracle. No other conceivable sacrifice could have caused him as much grief, and undoubtedly he had a dreadful struggle with himself before he could decide to do it. However, he won the struggle and having overcome his fear and doubt, through faith, it turned out that he did not have to make the sacrifice after all. On the contrary, an angel spoke to him and an extraordinary blessing, which he could never have expected, was bestowed upon him. "I will multiply thy seed as the stars of heaven and as the sand which is upon the seashore." This refers to future demonstrations or answers to prayer, and to rapid growth in spiritual understanding.

The above promise is followed by a still greater one, *"Thy seed shall possess the gate of his enemies."* You know that in the Bible enemies are always our fears and doubts, our troubles and problems. The gate was the most important place in the cities of the ancient world. The gate was where the enemies would naturally attack, and whoever possessed the gate would be in control of the city; and so you see the importance of this promise for the city which is your soul.

The account says that God tempted Abraham. Of course this is figurative. It was Abraham himself who had to prove his own faith.

If you are on the spiritual path there may be some particular thing which is keeping you back from demonstrating and from your overcoming. It may be anything, as no two people have quite the same weaknesses, but whatever it is it must go. Cost what it may *it must go.* Only thus can you prove your own faith, and then you will find it is no sacrifice at all, much as it seemed to be, but only the prelude to great triumph. Reread Genesis 22:1-18.

❧

A Member of the Audience

THERE ARE NO SHORT CUTS TO HEAVEN AND THE WAY to the Higher Consciousness is by taking yourself in hand. If you are in earnest, begin to watch yourself. Get off the stage of your life, and get into the audience. Watch yourself and be impartial in your judgments. Do not make excuses for yourself but do not be too harsh either in your opinions.

It does not matter where you stand today. The fact that I is watching Me means that you have taken one of the greatest steps forward. When you see yourself doing things that are useless, or perhaps even mean or petty, stop them. When you find that I can laugh at Me, it means that your life is commencing to change for the better. Finally, you will find that Me is beginning to get in step with I, and when that happens you are truly on the road to having dominion over your life.

There are no short cuts to Heaven but you can have fun changing your life over if you become a member of the audience.

❦

The Sunshine of God's Love

BEHIND EVERY PROBLEM OR DIFFICULTY LIES THE Truth of Being. This means that in spite of the appearance, you must believe that Divine Mind has already healed the situation—that in reality there is nothing but God, or good. Jesus referred to this when he said that when you pray, believe that you *have received*, and you shall receive. And at another time, he said, "The Father worketh hitherto and I work."

These statements by Jesus make it very clear that we do not deal with symptoms, but that we must work in our consciousness to lift it above and beyond the mere seeming to the love and goodness of God Himself.

Often, however, we are so close to a problem that, spiritually speaking, we accept the cloudy day as a permanent state of climate, forgetting that the sunshine of

Divine Love and Power has never ceased to shine, although obscured for the moment.

In prayer or treatment, we remind ourselves again that, no matter how bleak or overcast the picture may be, we believe that God has already healed the difficulty, that in Divine Mind there is nothing but good and therefore only good can express itself in these circumstances.

This is the basis of scientific prayer. What words you use, or what portions of the Bible you read, should depend entirely upon what appeals to you at the moment. The important thing is to raise your consciousness above the level where the difficulty seems to be. When you have wiped the problem out of your mind—and put God there instead—you will soon find that it has disappeared from the material world also.

Then shall the righteous shine forth as the sun in the kingdom of their Father (Matthew 13:43).

Persistence Brings Results

PRAYER IS THE ONE THING THAT CAN MAKE A CHANGE in your life. It matters not what your religion may be, or whether you adhere to none. If you will go direct to God in simple, affirmative prayer, you can heal your body, bring peace and harmony into your life, enlarge your social contacts, and make prosperity a reality.

Of course, those in the Truth teaching already know this, but sometimes discouragement sets in because the demonstration does not come immediately.

Now, if there is one rule we should make in regard to prayer, it is that we must be *persistent*. Of course, we should always feel that the prayer we are making is the one that will demonstrate, but we should also always be ready to pray again if the demonstration does not come.

Persistence in prayer is really only an expression of our abiding faith in God's love and goodness, for by our persistence we are affirming our belief that God does answer prayer.

Persistence in prayer always brings results.

Men ought always to pray, and not to faint.—Jesus Christ.

❧

Stake Your Claim!

IN THE OLD GOLD RUSH DAYS PROSPECTORS WENT OUT in the mountains in search of the yellow metal. Often the task was long and arduous with little to show for days of struggle and privation. But when a find was made, the prospector would stake his claim so that others would know that that particular discovery belonged to him. Of course, some claims turned out to be shallow veins of ore and worth little, while other claims eventually made their owners fabulously wealthy.

In metaphysics, we often speak of claiming our good, and it is one of the surest ways of bringing the good we desire into our lives. Unlike the prospector, however, when we stake our claim with God, we need have no anxiety about the results.

If you want health, then claim every day that God is your health, that as a child of God you have perfect health (the present temporary appearance notwithstanding), that Divine Life brings well-being to every part of your body.

If you want prosperity, then claim every day that God is your prosperity and the Giver of every good gift, that God knows you and is ready to more than supply your every need.

If you want peace and harmony, then claim every day that God brings you the peace that passeth all understanding, that all things work together for good to them that love God.

Whatever it is you wish to bring into your life, *stake your claim to it.*

Of course, we often claim negative things for ourselves without fully realizing it.

Every time you say, "My cold," "My headache," "My indigestion," you are claiming those things for yourself. It is no wonder that so many people demonstrate these things—because what one claims for himself he will eventually bring into his life.

Affirm your divine kinship. All that the Father hath of health, and happiness, and abundance, is yours—if you will *stake your claim with God*.

How Much Can God Do?

THE BIBLE TELLS US, AMONG OTHER THINGS, THAT God can heal us, that He can deliver us from our destructions, that He lifts up the weak, that He leads and guides us, and inspires us. It tells us that God is a mighty fortress.

But just how much can God do? Well, God can do *almost* anything. That may sound strange to those of us who have been taught—and that includes all students of the metaphysical teaching—that with God all things are

22

possible. But there are some things that God cannot do, and it is fortunate for us that this is true.

God is a God of love and rules by divine principle, and because this is so, He cannot change His nature. He cannot break Divine Law. He cannot make exceptions to the rule. He cannot bring disease, or suffering, or lack. If He could do these things, He would not be God at all. Instead, He would be more like an oriental potentate ruling by whimsy and caprice, and we would be no farther advanced spiritually than the cave man and the savage who placated unknown gods with sacrifice and weird rites.

But because God cannot change His nature and is always the loving Father, more ready to give than to receive, we can go to Him with full confidence, knowing that He will hear and answer prayer, not because we seek a special favor, but because as children of the Most High, it is our divine heritage.

How much can God do? God can solve our every problem. He can heal our bodies and our conditions. He can remove all fear, and doubt, and frustration. He can bring heaven here and now—not by breaking the Law, which is impossible to God—but by fulfilling it.

Open Thou mine eyes, that I may behold wondrous things out of Thy law (Psalm 119:18).

❧

Powerful Prayers

THE BIBLE IS A TREASURE HOUSE OF PRAYER AND meditation. You will find that the following will prove powerful in daily use. Select those that cover your need of the moment:

I and my Father are One. If I take the wings of the morning, and dwell in the uttermost parts of the sea; even there shall Thy hand lead me, and Thy right hand shall hold me.

When my soul fainted within me I remembered the Lord: and my prayer came in unto Thee. I will fear no evil: for Thou art with me. He is my refuge and my fortress: my God; in Him will I trust. I will rejoice in Thy salvation. By my God have I leaped over a wall.

God is not the Author of confusion, but of peace.

I will go before thee, and make the crooked places straight: I will break in pieces the gates of brass, and cut in sunder the bars of iron. A thousand shall fall at thy side, and ten thousand at thy right hand; but it shall not come nigh thee.

I will restore health unto thee, and I will heal thee of thy wounds. God is the health of my countenance.

There is no power but of God. God is Love. God is the strength of my heart. God is my strength and power, and He maketh my way perfect. He guideth my way in perfectness.

The Lord shall give that which is good, and our land shall yield her increase. Our sufficiency is of God. Riches and honor are with me: yea, durable riches and right-eousness.

My heart is glad and my glory rejoiceth. While I live will I praise the Lord: I will sing praise unto my God while I have any being.

When . . .

WHEN YOUR KNEES ARE KNOCKING TOGETHER, AND you do not know which way to turn—*think of God and His goodness.*

When your coffers are empty and prosperity seems out of the question—*give thanks for God's abundance.*

When you want peace of mind—*get away from things, and dwell upon the Presence of God instead.*

When your health is under par—*speak the healing Word as Jesus did.*

When you need inspiration—*browse through the Bible.*

When your faith is low—*remember the words of Jesus, believe that you have received and you shall receive.*

When the situation seems to need a miracle—*remember that nothing is too difficult for God, and that He is performing miracles every day.*

Always "make a joyful noise unto the Lord." Go to Him with praise and thanksgiving. If you can do it, this is the most powerful prayer of all.

What's in a Name?

SHAKESPEARE ASKED THAT QUESTION AND FOLLOWED it by saying, "Would not a rose, by any other name, smell as sweet?" Of course, the rose *would* smell as sweet, because it would continue to give forth the beauty and scent for which it was created. And no matter what appellation might be applied to it, it would keep right on expressing itself as God intended.

Now, it matters not what *your name* is so long as you are living to the highest you know, and are really putting God first. Then your name will be the name of something fine, and upright, and virtuous, because you will be building those qualities into your life.

The Bible pays a lot of attention to names. For instance, Isaiah, in speaking of the coming of Jesus Christ, says, "His name shall be called Wonderful, Counsellor, The Prince of Peace." And Jesus spoke of himself as the Son of Man, and the Son of God. Each of these names indicates a quality in which Jesus was outstanding. So throughout the Bible, the name always indicates the character and qualities of the person or thing.

Now, the Bible was written for *you* and about *you,* and every name written therein belongs to you at one time or another. You are Job in all his misery when you believe in the power of outer things to bring disease and suffering. You are Judas when you have betrayed your knowledge of the Truth, and choose the lower instead of the higher. And you are Jesus when, momentarily, you have risen in consciousness, and know at that instant that you and God are one.

What's in a name? It all depends on how you choose to live.

A Mental Experiment

TRY THIS EXPERIMENT TODAY. SELECT ONE PARTICU-lar thing in your life which is not going well and which you wish to make successful. Then treat it each day with selected thought. Spend from a quarter of an hour to half an hour reconsidering the matter in the light of your knowledge of God and of prayer. Remind yourself that harmony and true success are the divine purposes of your life. Remind yourself that this particular thing must come under that law. Realize that because there can be no exceptions to natural law, this thing cannot remain inharmonious or negative once you know the Truth about it. Realize that you are *now* knowing the Truth about it and claim that the Divine Power in you is now healing the condition completely and permanently.

Then give thanks for a complete demonstration. Give thanks, and try to *feel* thankful. Mentally act the part of a person who has received his demonstration and is filled with natural gratitude. Remember that praise and thanksgiving are the most powerful prayers of all. Do not treat the subject again until next day.

Next day, repeat your treatment, and so on each day until the demonstration comes.

The treatment, however, is only one half of the work. In between treatments you must keep your thought right concerning the problem. If it is possible to keep your thought off it altogether in the intervals between treating, so much the better. If for any reason this is not possible, either because you are very much worried concerning it or because the condition is one which you cannot really get away from, the thing to do is to handle it with right thought all day long. This is vital. You must not allow yourself to think wrongly concerning that subject under any circumstances. If other people speak negatively, you cannot help that but you are not obliged to agree with them mentally. Remember that it is your mental agreement or acceptance that controls your life.

This all-day-long guiding of your thought about a particular subject cannot fail to bring your demonstration if you are persistent.

A Job to Be Done

THERE'S A JOB TO BE DONE," WAS A COMMON EX-pression in the army during the last war, and it meant that the individual soldier, high or low, knew that there was a task to be accomplished regardless of personal sacrifice or the difficulties involved.

Now, each one of us has a job to do; not the job in the shop, or office, or factory, or home, for that is only a small part of the whole—our place in the economic stream—but each one of us has a job to do, and that is in the matter of living life itself.

It is a job that not only calls for the best use of the

talents and equipment that have been given us, but it is a job that must include prayer, and meditation, and communion with God.

You can make life harmonious and beautiful as you let God unfold more and more through you, as you look to Him for guidance and inspiration, as you really "practice the Presence of God" in your everyday life. Or you can make the job of living a miserable and hazardous one if you forget God and try to do it alone.

But do the job you must, and because God has given you free will, it is for you to make the choice as to how it is to be done.

My meditation of Him shall be sweet: I will be glad in the Lord (Psalm 104:34).

❧

An Act of God

LEGAL PHRASEOLOGY IN CONTRACTS AND OTHER DOCU- ments is full of the expression, "an act of God," and almost always it refers to something unpleasant and undesirable, such as cyclones, floods, and famine.

Now, like the legal pronouncements, we are often prone to blame God, but God does not bring any of these things about, for God is the author only of perfect good, and we should rightfully attribute to Him only that which is good. Bitter as the pill may be, it is man who brings these negative things upon himself by his own wrong thinking—by his hatreds, and fears, and resentments—for the outer conditions must correspond to the inner thought whether it be that of an individual, or the collective thought of a nation.

But there are many *acts of God*—and they are always for good—because God is constantly acting in and through each one of us when we associate ourselves in thought with Him.

When, as a result of prayer, your body is healed, or things that were going wrong come right, or you find that the way ahead opens out before you, then can you joyfully say, "It is an act of God. Praise be to the Lord."

Praise Him for His mighty acts (Psalm 150:2).

Thanksgiving

THANKSGIVING DAY IS A PURELY AMERICAN FESTIVAL. It dates back to the early settlers who gave thanks for the bountiful crops that meant health and well-being during the coming winter. And so down through the years a day has always been set aside so that Americans of all faiths might acknowledge to God the many blessings they have received.

Now, no one needs to wait for Thanksgiving Day to give thanks to God. Indeed, we should make praise and thanksgiving a regular part of our prayers.

You will remember that Jesus said, "What things soever ye desire, when ye pray, believe that ye receive them, and ye shall have them." It is quite obvious from this that if you really believe that you shall receive them, then you should not only give thanks after your good is at hand, but you should constantly show your faith in God by giving thanks for the blessings you expect to receive.

Indeed, this is the royal road to demonstration, because we are not only confirming to ourselves our complete faith in the power and goodness of God, but we are acknowledging the receipt of that good from the Giver of all perfect gifts, God Himself. With praise and thanksgiving all obstacles can be overcome.

Offer unto God thanksgiving; and pay thy vows unto the Most High (Psalm 50:14).

❧

The Greatest Temptation

Get thee behind me, Satan. LUKE 4:8

THIS HAS BEEN A FAVORITE PHRASE WITH MANY RE-
ligious people, especially those in orthodoxy, and
they have used it in a sincere attempt to push temptation of one kind or another behind them.

Jesus himself used the expression. The oriental
phraseology gives a vividness and flavor that is some-
what lacking in our modern concept of evil. But Jesus
fully understood its nature because in this connection,
he not only told his disciples "to worship the Lord Thy
God, and Him only shalt thou serve," but, speaking
directly of the devil, said, "thou savourest not the things
that be of God, but those that be of men."

In metaphysics, we know that "satan" or the "devil"
is really our own lower selves tempting us to think and
act negatively.

You may be tempted in many ways, but the greatest
temptation—and the most common one—is the tempta-

34

tion to try material steps first instead of going directly to God.

Often this comes about through our early training, and even when we have been in the Truth teaching for some time, the old habit persists, and we only try God after material steps have failed. There are even some who say, "Get thee behind me, Satan," and then wait to see if the devil won't rescue them.

But this is not the Jesus Christ teaching. You are following in His footsteps, when you say, "Get thee behind me, Satan. Thou savourest of the things that be of men."

God can and will solve this problem.

❧

Shack or Palace?

THERE IS NO USE IN SAYING EVERYTHING WILL BE all right. That is only wishful thinking. Everything will not be all right unless you think rightly. Thinking rightly, of course, means putting God into all your affairs.

35

For example, if you are living in a shack, it is not any good pretending that it is a palace. That is only being "Pollyanna," and will get you nowhere in the end. Cheap optimism is never spiritual. Realize that you are living in a shack, but claim the Presence of God and that God will guide you to something better.

The spiritual way is to recognize the conditions surrounding you, but to know that they are only the present picture—what your present mentality is outpicturing.

The second step is to sit down quietly each day and think about God. Claim that He is with you and working in your affairs. Realize that God can and will change your circumstances. Daily meditations of this kind will sooner or later change your circumstances and bring them into harmony with the Truth of Being which means happiness, harmony, and abundance.

It does not matter what your present circumstances may be, the important thing is to keep up your own interest, for God never loses His.

✺

With All Sails Set

GOD INTENDED US TO HAVE DOMINION OVER OUR lives, to be the captain of our souls. We should be active in the kind of activity we like. We should be associating with those whom we desire; and as the years go on we should become happier, healthier, and younger.

However, the human race has not done that and the metaphysical message comes to us to lead us back to the thing that God meant us to be.

Now, if we are to be captain of our souls then we must speak with authority, as Jesus did. Of course, one cannot speak with authority unless he knows who he is. Jesus put it very plainly—"If you abide in me [the Christ of God] and God in you." When you realize that, then you know who you really are—the son of God.

Of course, in the ship of life, you cannot make port unless all sails are set. You must pursue the spiritual life wholeheartedly. You cannot expect to reach port if you are faithful in your prayers and meditations for a time, and then for a time you forget God. You cannot expect to reach port if you constantly make excuses for yourself, or if you leave dark corners in your life.

You are the captain of your soul and proceeding with all sails set, when you have put your life on the Spiritual Basis, and can say with Jesus, "I and the Father are One. It is not I that doeth the works but the Father in me."

❧

The Bible Has an Answer

DON'T TRY TO STRADDLE THE FENCE. IF YOU WISH TO accomplish anything, you must be single minded. It will be going the long way around if you first turn left and then right when you really want to go straight ahead. Let nothing turn you from the path. The Bible says, *A double minded man is unstable in all his ways.*

Don't spread gossip and criticism. You are doing the "devil's" work when you use these weapons, and he always pays off in kind. The Bible says, *Ye shall know the truth, and the truth shall make you free.*

Don't let change fill you with fear. Change is the order of the universe, for without change there can be no progress. Change is the very thing that most people need because it brings health, harmony, and prosperity to those who hold steadfastly to God. The Bible says, *The Lord is my rock, and my fortress.*

Don't let other people's problems influence your faith in the power and goodness of God. Pray for them if they ask you, but remember that each one is the captain of his own soul. The Bible says, *A thousand shall fall at thy side . . . but it shall not come nigh thee.*

Don't harbor superstitions of any kind, big or little. People often make a fetish of a number, or a date, or a keepsake; or they believe certain things bring "bad luck." This is denying God. The Bible says, *Thou shalt have no other gods before me. Because thou hast made the Lord, thy habitation; there shall no evil befall thee.*

❧

How Much Do You Demonstrate?

FROM TIME TO TIME PEOPLE HAVE COME TO ME AND said, "I am very enthusiastic about the teaching but I do not seem to demonstrate."

Of course, most of these people really are demonstrating all the time. They are demonstrating in accordance with their inner convictions. The point is a subtle one because outwardly they may desire a certain thing, but inwardly they have a fear of demonstrating it.

I knew of a man who kept looking for a job. He needed a job but could not demonstrate one. It was not until his second visit to my office that he confided that when he went for an interview with a prospective employer, although he needed the job, underneath he was afraid the other man might say yes.

Another case that comes to mind is that of a singer who gave auditions and wanted to sing, but always at the back of her mind was the fear that she might be accepted!

We are constantly balancing our "outer" desires by our inner negative thoughts and feelings with the consequence that we do not demonstrate the things we would like to have.

It is only when you rid your mind of these negative feelings that you will begin to demonstrate the things that you really desire. Let no little "devils" cancel out your treatments.

I will fear no evil: for Thou art with me (Psalm 23).

❧

What Do You See?

WHAT DO YOU COMMONLY SEE IN LIFE? ARE YOU constantly witnessing error and negative things? Or, do you bear testimony of the inherent goodness of God and His creation?

These are important questions because by your answers you can get a better understanding of yourself.

What we see in the outer is but a reflection of the inner, because we surround ourselves with a picture of our own beliefs. In other words, we manifest in general what we seriously think and believe.

So if we want to find out what our habitual thinking is like, we have but to look around us and ask ourselves what we really see.

The Bible says that we shall not bear false witness, but that is just what we are doing, for example, when we do not see the presence of God in every situation, or when we accept the appearance for the reality.

On the other hand, we are a witness for God, when we see the "whole" man where the sick one seems to be;

when we forgive someone who has injured us and then see the Christ in him; when we see prosperity instead of lack, knowing that God supplies every need; or when we see harmony and peace regardless of seeming outer conditions.

Perhaps you will recall the lines of Shakespeare: *there is nothing good or bad but thinking makes it so*

Are you seeing good everywhere? If not, start today to train yourself. You will be surprised to find how soon your own life will change for the better.

Count Your Blessings

WHEN THE YEAR IS NEARING ITS CLOSE, IT IS A GOOD time for us to take stock of the blessings we have received during the year.

As we look back over the year, we can see that there was many a blessing "in disguise" which we would have recognized at the time had we gotten behind the appearance to the reality of God.

Now, in taking stock of your demonstrations, do not rehash old difficulties, problems, and grievances. Remember this is to be an inventory of the good you have received, not a rehearsal of past mistakes. Then, when you have counted your blessings, if you feel that you could have done better, take a step farther.

In the commercial field, a firm takes an inventory not only to find out what goods it has on hand, but also to see if it cannot improve its business through more judicious merchandising.

Likewise in your spiritual inventory, you should use it as a basis for making further progress. You can take a step forward by asking yourself:

1. When a problem arises do I "Golden Key"* the situation by seeing God where the trouble seems to be?

2. Have I gotten rid of anger, fear, and resentment?

3. Have I forgiven everyone whom I think has injured me? Jesus made this one of the cardinal points in the great Lord's Prayer. We are to ask God to forgive us as we have forgiven others.

If you put these things into practice, then next year at this time your spiritual inventory will reflect the difference, for there will be many more blessings to count.

* See booklet, "The Golden Key."

A Door Opens

CHANGE IS THE LAW OF THE UNIVERSE. WITHOUT change, the world would not merely remain in a static state, but it would soon become stale and stagnant. Without change there would be no progress, for change is the very essence of every betterment. It is quite obvious that to do anything in a new and better way there must be a change.

Yet many people look upon any change that comes into their lives with dread and foreboding. But for those on the spiritual path—for those who believe in God and the power of prayer—change is an invitation to the fuller expression of life. It means that a new door has opened and you are ready to take a step forward.

Paul tells us in his epistle to the Romans that we are to be transformed by the renewing of our minds in order that we may more fully do God's will. In this statement he really suggests that not only should we not fear change but rather that we should actively bring it about by the renewing or changing of our minds. By doing

44

this, he says that we shall be transformed. In other words, our old problems and difficulties shall fade away, and like the butterfly that emerges from its confining chrysalis, we shall experience a new freedom and a new joy.

When a problem or condition arises in your life that indicates a change, rely upon God, and realize that it is not so much that a door has closed on a chapter of your life, but rather that a door has opened on new and more interesting things.

Remember that the Bible does not say, "Cling to the old"—it says, "Behold, I make all things new."

Use That Broom!

A GOOD HOUSEKEEPER SEES TO IT THAT DUST AND DIRT do not accumulate in nooks and corners and on shelves. Periodically, the house is gone over and given a thorough cleaning.

Too often in our spiritual lives, we allow negative things to accumulate in the corners of our minds. We tackle the obvious problems as they come along, but allow the small difficulties to pile up in the corners, or perhaps push them down into the subconscious, and try to forget about them.

For instance, if you are faced with a problem of health or finance, you will get to work on that immediately, but if, on the other hand, someone has injured you, instead of handling it spiritually at the time, you probably tuck it away in your mind, and perhaps pack in a little resentment along with it.

And so with many problems of a like nature, such as envy, jealousy, false pride, and various faults of character. These should be dealt with as they arise. But in any case, if you have allowed them to accumulate, now is the accepted time to sweep them out of the corners where they have piled up.

If someone has injured you, forgive him now, and be done with it. Or if you have injured someone else, ask God's forgiveness, and claim His blessing on the other person as well as on yourself. Take care of the other difficulties in like manner.

Be a good housekeeper. Do not sweep these negative things "under the carpet" for they will only be there to plague you later on. Clean out every nook and corner—and God will make you worthy of greater accomplishments in the future, because your house will be founded upon the rock of Truth, and nothing else.

✣

Unprofitable Talk

*Should a wise man utter vain knowledge, and
fill his belly with the east wind?*

*Should he reason with unprofitable talk? or
with speeches wherewith he can do no good?*
                                        JOB 15:2, 3

THERE ARE OCCASIONS WHEN DIFFICULTIES SEEM TO
hang on with little or no improvement. At such
times one is perhaps tempted to forsake his knowledge of
Truth, and say, "What is the use? I don't seem to get
any results from prayer." If we continue in that state of
mind, we soon go through a period of depression and
despair, and we create a negative cycle where difficulty
piles on difficulty.

Of course, it is easy to see why this should happen
because negative thinking only begets more negative
thinking, and we simply keep on producing more and
more negative conditions.

Now, prayer is always good, but it is at the very times
that we think prayer is not working that we need it most.

Instead of going round and round like a trapped rat

47

in a cage, you should pause and reflect once more upon the love and goodness of God, because it is only by a rise in consciousness that you can begin to rise above your problems.

Having taken this initial step, seek to give your prayers a freshness by reading something in the Bible or some good spiritual book. Get away from hackneyed affirmations that you have come to recite parrot fashion. Talk to God like a little child in simplicity and faith.

Then forget about your difficulties for the time being, leaving the results to God. Do not look forward to another treatment because this is only affirming that the present one will not work; but pray again later on if you find it necessary.

If thou return to the Almighty, thou shalt be built up (Job 22:23).

The Fourth Man

WHEN NEBUCHADNEZZAR SENT OUT HIS DECREE that everyone in his kingdom should bow down and worship the golden image which he had erected, there were three men who refused to obey his edict. These were Shadrach, Meshach, and Abed-nego. They were officials in the province of Babylon, and had much to lose by their refusal.

Nebuchadnezzar called them before him, and they bluntly told the king that their God would deliver them from the fiery furnace to which they would be consigned, but that even if God did not deliver them, they would still serve Him and Him alone.

Now, so long as you believe in God only and worship Him for His own sake, you can expect to be delivered from the ills and miseries that beset mankind. Of course, every Christian will say, "Naturally, I believe in God only. I do not worship idols or golden images. So this does not affect me." However, if you give power to sin, sickness, or evil of any kind, by believing in it, or if you think an advantage can be gained by distorting the truth, then you have made idols of these things, and in that sense, worship them.

Well, Nebuchadnezzar had the three men thrust into the fiery furnace, and the heat was so intense that it slew the guards that threw them in. And, as he looked, Nebuchadnezzar was astonished to find a *fourth man* walking in the flames with the other three, and he *knew* that this one was like unto the Son of God. Then Shadrach, Meshach, and Abed-nego walked out of the fiery furnace without blemish or scar.

So it is when we hold steadfastly to God, and give all power to Him. He sends his messenger, the Christ truth, to heal us and deliver us from our furnace of fear and frustration. Then do we know that nothing shall by any means hurt us.

Blessed be God . . . Who hath sent His angel, and delivered His servants that trusted in Him (Daniel 3:28).

❦

Holiness Unto the Lord

THIS PHRASE IS USED SEVERAL TIMES IN THE BIBLE,[*] and in our ordinary King James Version the whole phrase is always printed in capitals, indicating unusual importance. Now what do these very important words mean? Well, they contain nothing less than the master key to life.

Holiness unto the Lord means that there is nothing in existence but the self-expression of God—that and

* Exodus 39:30, Zechariah 14:20, and elsewhere.

nothing more. It naturally follows from this that you yourself, and every condition in your life today, are simply part of God's manifestation or self-expression, and therefore must be perfect, beautiful, and harmonious. It may not seem so to the limited human mind, but nevertheless it is the Truth of Being.

This is not a mere abstract truth, but is an extremely practical matter, because to know this and to have faith in it rapidly clears up any kind of difficulty that may be in your life. Instead of a mere academic speculation it is the most powerful healing agent in existence. It will heal the body, readjust every kind of difficulty with other people, solve all business troubles, bring you inspiration and courage, and move you into your true place if you have not already found it.

These words were written upon a golden crown which surmounted the headdress of the high priest, and a later prophecy says that in the day of triumph these words shall be upon the bells of the horses. Of course, you yourself are really a high priest, as Aaron was, when you are engaged in realizing the presence of God where a negative condition seems to be, and it is in your day of triumph (when your prayer is answered) that the words will be seen upon the bells of the horses. You know those horses* and at that time the three inferior horses will have been redeemed forever.

A bell is a proclamation; a summons. Church bells are rung to proclaim that a church service is about to be held and to summon the people. And bells used for secular purposes have the same essential significance. The bells on your horses will proclaim the power of prayer and will summon other people to the Higher Thought because when they see the changes that have come over you they will hasten to obtain the same blessings.

Do not accept trouble at its face value. Realize the *holiness* of God where the trouble seems to be. Have faith in it, and all will be well.

Your Master Demonstration

THERE ARE TWO OR THREE FUNDAMENTAL PRINCI-ples with which we are all acquainted, and in which we believe—at least in theory. Unfortunately, however, there are still many people who give assent to these prin-

* See booklet, "The Four Horsemen of the Apocalypse."

ciples but yet realize them only slightly. Of course, there are also some who have at least a fair realization of what they mean, but not one of us has anything like a full realization.

As soon as we succeed in getting a strong realization (even though not 100 per cent) things will begin to move for the better in our lives with a power and rapidity that we have not yet even dreamed of.

The first thing you must begin to realize is that there is nothing that prayer cannot accomplish. Many people are perfectly ready to accept these principles as theories but they think that even if they could be made to work, the task would call for extraordinary and exceptional beings. But you have to know that you must begin to realize not only that they apply to you personally but that *your own prayers* can work the miracle. So this applies not only to the prayers of others for you but to *your own prayers* for yourself or for your loved ones. This is true because it is God who is the Healer, and the potency of your prayer will depend solely on the faith that you put into it and not upon any other quality.

These things being true—and they are—I am going to suggest that you personally, whoever you are who is reading this, begin to work along these lines immediately. By this I mean, naturally, that you will begin to

53

work for greater *realization* of the fundamental truths quoted above, and not be satisfied to say that you already know them and accept them.

Most of you have had at least one or two very remarkable demonstrations, or answers to prayer, but in most cases they have happened only occasionally. Now begin to make them occur more and more often, and determine also to make your Master Demonstration this year.

By the Master Demonstration of your life I mean demonstrating whatever is most important in your life; by far more important than anything else whatever. When you succeed in that it will in itself naturally change your life infinitely for good, and apart from the actual demonstration you will find that you have taken an incalculable step forward on the spiritual path.

Watch Your Step!

Keep thy foot when thou goest to the house of God, and be more ready to hear, than to give the sacrifice of fools: for they consider not that they do evil.   ECCLESIASTES 5:1

THIS CHAPTER, FROM WHICH THE ABOVE VERSE IS taken, is really a treatise on the art of living; and here in the first verse the Bible writer sums up his message.

He begins by saying, "Keep thy foot," which is a strange expression to us. Nowadays we would say, "Watch your step," but as with all the Bible teaching there is an inner meaning too. The foot, in the Bible, stands for spiritual understanding, and so to "keep thy foot" means to maintain your spiritual understanding.

"To go to the house of God" does not mean merely to go into a particular church or building. You go to the house of God when you remember that God is also present, no matter where you may be. So the Bible writer says, in effect, that if you maintain your spiritual understanding and remember that God is present where you are, you will be "more ready to hear"—to receive your revelation or inspiration from God.

"To give the sacrifice of fools" is to accept things because someone else has told you rather than to get your inspiration direct from God. "For they consider not that they do evil" means that man's thoughts are often negative, and negative thoughts can only bring trouble in their wake.

To sum it up, we are told in this verse that if we want to be successful in life, to have spiritual understanding, and direct inspiration from God Himself, we must practice the Presence of God. To listen to any other voice than His can only be a snare and a deceit.

The Gold Mine Within

ALL THROUGH HISTORY THE IDEA OF THE GOLD MINE has intrigued the imagination and given men interest, and where there is interest, there is power. In the Bible too, gold symbolizes power—the omnipresence of Divine Power.

You have a gold mine within more fabulous than the famous mines of King Solomon, or any of those that have been discovered in the Klondike, or California, or the Rand. Of course, the gold mine within does not mean within the body. It certainly does not mean within in any physical sense.

In metaphysics, or the Truth teaching, when we speak of "within" we mean thought. "Without" or "outside" means expression or manifestation. For instance, we sometimes say, "As within, so without," meaning that as we think so do we express.

So the gold mine within means that your power in life lies in your thought. However, to operate this gold mine you need a contact with God. It will be of little avail to reach out for it without that.

Your contact with God lies in recognizing your identity, the "I am." The "I am" is everything you arrogate to yourself in thought. If you say, "I am sick," you have ordered your own. If you say, "I am well, I am one with God," you have ordered your own.

God is universal—"I am that I am"—and you as an individual particularize it when you say, "I am." When you use your "I am" in an inverted or negative sense, you are using it against yourself and will bring sickness, poverty, controversy, and fear into your life.

When you particularize, or individualize, Divine Power by using your "I am" constructively, then you will get health, prosperity, and abounding happiness, for you will have identified yourself with God—the gold mine within.

❧

The Middle Wall of Partition

For He is our peace, Who hath made both one, and hath broken down the middle wall of partition between us.   EPHESIANS 2:14

I THINK THAT THIS IS NOT ONLY ONE OF THE MOST beautiful texts in the Bible, but one of the most important also. Yet it is not one of the best known texts. Of course, all good Bible students have read it many times in going through this chapter, but I wonder how many of them have studied and realized the full import of it. I think that very many have read it only perfunctorily and passed on to another verse that seemed better known and more obvious.

Yet, what statement of Truth could be more obvious, and more telling, if you give your mind to it.

58

Consider what it says. It says that God is our peace, and we all know that peace of mind is the most important and most powerful of all things. It says that *He,* God, is our peace and not we ourselves. This phrase alone cuts out any personal effort or struggle on our own part, for these are the things that spoil our prayers. As long as we think that we are doing it, and that we must struggle to get higher in consciousness, and select just the right phrases, and above all, that we must expect to wait until we are much better and have much more understanding, we are likely to wait indefinitely. All these things make us tense and anxious, and turn us away from God. And yet, this is just what so many sincere people do.

Next the verse says that not only are we and God one (all spiritual teachers say that) but that it is He who has made us one, and not ourselves as the result of hard work. We are One because that is the nature of being since He has made us that way.

The verse goes on to say that He has broken down the middle wall of partition between us. What could be more graphic or dramatic than this? The inspired writer here uses a figure of speech. He reminds us that when we lose our sense of unity with God, it is exactly as though a wall were built between God and ourselves, or, let us say, between two people. When that happens the communication is broken, and we are no longer one in consciousness, until, of course, the wall is pulled down. But, the verse teaches that it is God who pulls the wall down—and who will doubt that God can do it? Then we will once more experience our contact, and our problem will promptly begin to fade out, and God's inspiration will come back.

In any difficulty the one important thing is to have the temporary wall of partition pulled down, and to let God do it—for only He can.

❧

Your Daily Visit with God

WHO IS OUR PEACE? OF COURSE, WE ALL KNOW THAT it is God alone who is our peace—although nearly all of us tend to forget it from time to time, however heartily we believe it. Our tendency is, occasionally at least, without realizing it, to rest upon ourselves, which means, of course, that we think that we are our own peace. We would never admit this to ourselves, but it happens, and the only result is that we get no results until we change that attitude.

As soon as we begin to think like that, we shall quickly realize it because things will start to go wrong, or we shall begin to feel a little depressed. Then, of course, we must remind ourselves that it is God who is our peace, and put our confidence in Him; in other words, *rest on the lord*.

These mistakes occur from time to time, because we have been neglecting our daily visit with God. That visit can be prayer, meditation, spiritual reading, or any other spiritual exercise.

This daily visit is the greatest possible investment that you could make with your time—the ten or fifteen minutes, or half hour, whichever suits you best. Ask yourself what else you could possibly do with that time that would be of greater value, or really help you more. And yet people frequently postpone it because they tell themselves that they haven't time today, or have something much more urgent or important to do.

Now, when you think that you are too busy for your daily visit, let me ask you frankly, what wonderful thing are you doing that is more important? Obviously there could not be anything nearly as important as your daily visit with God. No matter what the other thing is it cannot be as important as that. There is nothing that you could possibly do with that time which would bring you greater benefit in every respect. As a matter of fact, if you have something very important and urgent to do you will always be able to find time to do it and to have your visit too. And your visit will make that very important thing go through much more easily and successfully.

Nearly always when some one tells himself that he has to neglect his daily visit because there is something urgent and important that must be done instead, the truth is that he has wasted that amount of time on things of no importance.

Neglect anything else if you must, but do not neglect your daily visit with God.

Acquaint now thyself with Him and be at peace.

❦

Realization Is the Key

IF THERE IS A PARTICULAR TRUTH THAT YOU DO NOT truly realize—then it does not belong to you. It will belong to you as soon as you realize it; but not before. This is why most spiritual teachers tell their students that they must do the work for themselves in the long run. Of course, people in special difficulties do need help from someone else occasionally and they should never hesitate to ask for it, but still the fact remains that we must do our own work as a rule.

The old-fashioned habit of telephoning a healer every time some minor thing went wrong, was mistaken, and is now dying out.

The moment that you realize a particular Truth, it begins to work in your life. It begins to change, first your consciousness, and then your body or outer circumstances. You know, of course, that outer things always follow the consciousness.

But any spiritual Truth that you begin to realize at least to some extent, will go far beyond this. It not only changes and heals the particular problem for which you were praying, but it will change every part of your nature for the better.

Often you will suddenly come to a realization of something you never understood before. An entirely new meaning of a particular text will open out to you. That text was familiar and you thought you understood it but now you get something new, and you will think, with surprise and joy, "Oh, that is the full meaning! It never occurred to me before." This is a great step forward in understanding and naturally it brings some kind

63

of healing, because we cannot get an increase in understanding without getting a healing also. It may not necessarily be a physical healing. It may be a healing of your disposition, or an increase in Divine Love, or the overcoming of a fault, and so forth. And whatever the new thing is, you will never lose it again.

Realization is the key to demonstration.

❦

Resting on God

NEVER FORGET THAT ONCE GOD DOES HIS WORK IN you, you never lose it. It is a permanent change in you.

It often happens that when you learn a secular subject and perhaps master it for the time being, later on you will find that you have forgotten it, especially if you have not kept in touch with it—but you never lose anything that comes to you along spiritual lines.

You may forget it from time to time, for that is very human, but then before long you will find yourself in difficulties again and that reminds you, and you think,

"That was the mistake that I made before"; and you promptly turn to God once more and you regain your contact with Him, and the trouble disappears. By now you have learned through experience not to try to do these things yourself but you simply *see God doing them*. This is one of the most important points concerning prayer.

The most powerful prayer is simply to see God doing the work and to rejoice in this. This is the best way of all to avoid tension and will power, and therefore to get results.

When we turn back to God in our hearts, and that is what we are doing in times like this, the power of God immediately begins to express itself in our lives. Fear begins to go and then the demonstration comes.

Never forget that only God can answer prayer—we cannot. It would probably be safe to say that the reason why most people do not get answers to their prayers is that they pray too hard. This is not leaving it to God, which is the only way to get results.

Remember that the basic and only sin is fundamentally a lack of faith in God. The only thing that really matters is to give all power to God at all times—and watch yourself (without anxiety) to see that you really are giving all power to Him. When you do this, fear begins to fade out. It is said a number of times in the Old Testament, "They limited the Holy One."

It is a very good thing that when we forget God for a time, or do not give Him all power, that troubles come. If they did not we would go on doing these things indefinitely. The fact that trouble follows whenever we forget God or cease to give Him all power, is the greatest blessing that the human race has. This fact is what keeps many people from slipping away altogether.

Anything that brings us back to God is entirely good.

Seeking and Finding

PEOPLE ARE VERY APT TO FIND WHAT THEY SEEK. In fact, there is a cosmic law that tends to make this happen. Of course, it does not always happen but such is the tendency.

You have certainly noticed that people who go about looking for trouble, practically always find it. The popular proverb, "Listeners never hear good of themselves," is an example of this tendency. In metaphysics we know that the pessimist is defeated before he starts. We have all known people who loved to say that they never have any luck. When things seem to go against them, they will exclaim triumphantly, "Wouldn't you know it?— that is what always happens to me!" And needless to say, their personal affairs constantly do go wrong.

Now, such a mistaken person has only got to alter this habit and he will automatically Alter His Life. It is often difficult to get such people to make this alteration but if they do, the result is never in doubt.

The spiritual teaching tells us that conditions and tendencies can always be changed by a change in our own convictions. Spiritual law says that it is never too late to mend and that the hand of God Himself is always outstretched to put us triumphantly on our feet if we will turn to Him.

Look unto Me all ye ends of the earth, for I am the Lord, and there is none other.

✣

That Illogical Fellow

PEOPLE SOMETIMES SAY, "I BELIEVE FIRMLY IN THE spiritual teaching, and I have done so for years, but I have never been able to make it work—isn't that strange?" And sometimes they say this with quite an air of triumph.

Such people remind me of a certain man who used to boast that he had an ailment that no one could heal. It seems that he had successfully defied every school of healing known to the public and had emerged triumphantly still in possession of his affliction. As it happens, his wife did heal him later on by prayer alone, but she was a patient and persevering woman.

Of course, if you go about saying or thinking that you cannot make the teaching work (which usually means that you do not expect to) you are really making a law for yourself to that effect, and you should never be tired of reminding yourself that when you make a mental law for yourself you do have to live under it. You may have known this law for forty or fifty years and yet, being human, you are likely to forget it, at least occasionally.

That man's wife probably points the way to the overcoming of this mistake. The key to success with such problems lies in just the qualities that she obviously had; patience combined with a gentle and unhurried expectation of success.

The patient whom she healed is not a rare specimen, nor is he unknown to anyone. We are all likely to encounter him under our own hat at any moment!

68

How to Do It!

INSIST on peace of mind, health, and happiness; these things are God's will for you.

RESIGNATION IS REALLY A SIN—BUT DO NOT BE TOO impatient either.

If an old problem continues to stick—pray for inspiration and intelligence.

If everything seems to be sticking—stop struggling and thank God constantly for setting you free. Use this treatment exclusively for a week or so.

If you feel depressed or discouraged—work to realize Life and Joy, and give thanks for these things.

If nervous or frightened—throw the responsibility on God, and tell Him that you know you are safe in His hands.

If someone is being troublesome—see only the Presence of God where the troublesome person seems to be.

If you want to make faster progress—claim understanding and affirm that Divine Love is working through you.

The Man Who Lived One Day

ONE OF THE MOST IMPORTANT RULES IN META-
physics is to live in the present. Live in today,
and do not allow yourself to live in the past under any
pretense. Living in the past means thinking about the
past, rehearsing past events, especially if you do this
with feeling.

The carnal mind is very anxious to make us live in
the past—and it is extraordinarily cunning in getting us
to do this even though we do not want to. It finds the
most plausible excuses to make us think back, so that
many intelligent people tell themselves, "I must not
dwell on the past, I know, but in this case there is a
good reason." Of course, this is ridiculous. There is
never a good reason.

It does not make much *fundamental* difference
whether you are thinking of pleasant things in the past
or unpleasant—although, needless to say, thinking of
pleasant things is much better than thinking of troubles
or griefs—but still, thinking of the past at all is still

thinking of the past and that delays our progress and makes it much harder to demonstrate.

Live in today, and instead of thinking about pleasant things in the past, think of pleasant things today, or if things seem to be going badly at the moment, think that God is putting them right and that very soon you will be happy and satisfied. If you think this with faith and conviction it will come about, and the more conviction you put into these thoughts the faster it will come about. In this way you will make today, or at least the very near future, joyous and successful—this will really happen.

Now, is not this much better than thinking of even very happy things in the past; which are still, after all, dead and gone, and out of reach? Of course, rehearsing past troubles, disappointments, etc., is simply creating much more trouble. Ideally, a student of metaphysics should live one day only at a time—that is the present day. If he does that, tomorrow, when it comes, will be very happy and successful.

Needless to say, the carnal mind is simply your lower self including all fears and bad habits of thought that you have picked up in the course of your life. It is not intelligent. It is simply negative habits working themselves out.

Train yourself to be a man or woman who lives one

day—at a time. You will be surprised how rapidly conditions will change for the better when you approach this ideal. You can lose nothing and will gain much. Does not the Bible say:

Behold, now is the accepted time; behold, now is the day of salvation.

🌺

Basic Principles

FROM A TRUE UNDERSTANDING OF METAPHYSICS WE learn that God as Cause is perfect, that he individualizes Himself as man, and that man by the exercise of his free will, can create or think good or evil.

If man thinks thoughts of good, he is working in harmony with Divine Law, and good follows: If he thinks thoughts of error, he limits in his own experience the full expression of God, and he experiences evil—and he must go on experiencing it as long as he continues to think limitation.

We learn further that good, which is the expression of God, is unchanging and eternal; whereas error thoughts, though they cause pain and suffering for the moment, have no true substance (or to use a technical term, "reality"), and therefore can be destroyed, or made to cease to exist.

Notice particularly that correct metaphysical science does not deny the existence of the physical world, but teaches that our understanding of it is limited, faulty, and changing. From this it follows that our duty, as well as our self-interest, demands that we work upon our consciousness until we produce a correct understanding which will mean for us the end of sin, sickness, and death.

Judge not according to the appearance, but judge righteous judgment (John 7:24).

❧

There Is Nothing But God

MOST PEOPLE WHO ARE IN TRUTH KNOW, AT LEAST theoretically, that when a difficulty suddenly arises, the important thing is to switch one's thought immediately from the difficulty to the Presence of God.

But in practice, this procedure is not always so easy of accomplishment. Too often when we are confronted

73

with an unexpected difficulty, in common with those who are not in Truth, we hit back at the error. Of course, this is exactly what we should not do. We can get nowhere by fighting error with error. Instead, we must switch our thought—as quickly as possible—away from the appearance to the Presence of God. The Bible calls this fleeing to the mountains.

Now, it does not matter just how you do this. You might find it best to think promptly of God, or recite a favorite verse from the Bible.

But perhaps for most people, the quickest and surest way is simply to say to oneself, *there is nothing but God,* repeating this several times, if necessary.

Of course, you should acquaint yourself beforehand with just what you mean by this statement so that it will have a vital significance for you.

Behold upon the mountains the feet of Him that bringeth good tidings, that publisheth peace! (Nahum 1:15).

Setting-Up Exercises

E VERYONE TODAY KNOWS THAT THE BODY HAS TO BE exercised if we want to be healthy. An athlete must go into training and tune up his body if he wishes to be successful. Most people, too, know that any particular muscle and most organs will respond to special exercises. They will become stronger, or healthier, and above all, the owner will get much more control over them.

Every musician has to practice constantly for two reasons. First, he develops the part of the body concerned, be he a singer, a violinist, or a pianist, and at the same time he gains that real control, over whichever is his instrument, that is essential to success.

All this is equally true in the spiritual life. You must practice. And the only way to practice is by trying to solve your problems with prayer. This develops your spiritual power and it also trains you to use that spiritual power in the most effective way.

Neglecting your prayers and your visit with God, or

trying to get some one else to solve all your problems, will never develop your own spiritual faculty.

Whatever you do you should never neglect your regular spiritual setting-up exercises.

Draw nigh to God, and He will draw nigh to you.

꽃

Four Little Words

THY WILL BE DONE. THIS IS ONE OF THE MOST familiar phrases used in the Christian religion. It is naturally a quotation from the Lord's Prayer that everyone has learned in childhood. I doubt if any other text from the Bible is used more frequently.

It is a most powerful and inspiring prayer—if it is used in the correct sense, that is, with true understanding of its meaning. In that case there could be no greater or more important prayer; and obviously it takes less than a minute to repeat it once, although of course, you can repeat it as often as you feel led to do.

Unfortunately, however, it seems that comparatively few people ever do use it with correct understanding; in spite of their very good intentions. In such cases, it is of very little practical use, and occasionally may even do a certain amount of harm.

These results arise from the fact that so many excellent people when they use this prayer assume (perhaps without always realizing the fact) that the Will of God is sure to be something sad, or even unpleasant.

In this instance they are using the words from a lofty though mistaken sense of duty. They mean that they are perfectly willing that the Will of God shall be done even though it involves suffering for them or others.

The truth is, naturally, that the Will of God will *always* be something good, and joyous, and inspiring, for every human being, because we know that God wishes only these things for His children. Therefore, when we say *Thy Will be done,* with understanding, we are praying for those very things, and God will bring them into our own lives, or into the lives of those for whom we are praying. This prayer, only four little words, will wipe out the trouble whatever it is, and bring comfort and healing in its place.

Of course, when people use those words in the negative sense they are believing in the reality of trouble, and expecting it to continue or even increase—and we know that whatever we really believe in or expect, will happen to us.

Train yourself to use these words in the true sense and you will have acquired an invincible weapon against difficulties.

❧

Praying with a Feather

YEARS AGO MANY DEVOTED PREACHERS AND SUNDAY School teachers were fond of telling people to "pray hard." Well meaning as this advice was, it was mistaken. I often tell people to pray "soft" which, of course, means gently.

I do this because I know that the more quietly and gently we pray, the better results do we get. In prayer, as in many other activities, effort defeats itself.

More than once, on the platform, I have said to my congregation, "Pray with a feather—not with a pickax." This always makes people smile (which is why I say it) and that means that it is going to make a more vivid impression on them, and that they are sure to remember it much longer than if I had expressed it in a formal way.

Always pray gently, and especially if you have a good deal of fear, or your difficulty seems to be a very important one.

❧

Peace, the Miracle Worker

REGENERATION MEANS BUILDING A NEW MENTALITY; that is, creating a new soul in place of your present one. It does not mean merely improving your present self —it means producing (through the power of God, of course), a new self.

If you do this, everything else in your life will rapidly change for the better. Your health will improve. Your appearance will improve because, as you know, the body is but the reflection of the soul. The world around you will be changed because you will be seeing it through a new and better personality. Other people will become much more attractive and friendly to you, and this will be because your soul will be filled with peace, and therefore you will radiate peace, and other people will get it intuitively. Everybody likes peace and harmony and they are attracted to any source from which it comes.

If your heart really is filled with peace "nothing shall by any means hurt you." But, of course, your heart must be filled with peace and to bring this about you must desire it more than anything else. This will mean forgiving everyone and harboring good will toward all.

Naturally you cannot radiate peace if you do not first possess it within yourself. You cannot radiate anything from the outside. To radiate any quality, that quality must be within yourself. Hypocrites sometimes try to radiate qualities which they do not possess or feel, but they always fail to get results in a very short time.

True peace of mind is *the* short cut to regeneration which requires a fundamental change in ourselves.

The Master said, *Peace I leave with you; my peace I give unto you.*

With God All Things Are Possible*

THIS IS ONE OF THE BEST KNOWN TEXTS IN THE BIBLE —and one of the most misunderstood.

Almost everyone takes it to mean simply that God, being omnipotent, can do anything He wants to. Natu-

* Matthew 19:26.

rally, that is perfectly true, but if this were all that the text meant Jesus would probably not have taken the trouble to say it, for it would have no practical application in the lives of men and women. People would think, "Certainly it is true, but how do I know God will choose to do this thing for me?"

When we understand the real meaning of this text it springs to life at once and becomes the most important thing we know.

The text really means that all things are possible to you when God is working *with* you. In other words, when you are working with God all things are possible.

God always works with you when you ask Him to and when you have faith that He is doing so. Then your prayer cannot fail. It is God who is changing things and not you.

He careth for you.

You Must Cultivate Poise

POISE IS A MARK OF THE SPIRITUAL LIFE. IN ADDITION, it is the key to happiness.

Most people have at least a vague understanding of this truth. They would like to have poise very much—but they do not know how to go about getting it. They say, "I wish I could be poised at all times, or at least, most times, but *how to bring it about?*" Sometimes they say, "I have worked very hard to get it; in fact, occasionally I have worked so hard for it that I am quite tired out." Of course, working hard is itself a negation of poise; it is tenseness.

When you have poise, everything in your life comes easily, and you see how to solve a problem even without special prayer for that difficulty. Indeed, you often find yourself saying or doing the right thing almost automatically. Certainly your prayers have far more power when you are poised.

Here is the technique for acquiring poise. First, stop hurrying. Do what is necessary but without rushing. Secondly, train yourself to think only of what you want to think of at the time. Thirdly, make it a rule to keep your mind where you are, or on whatever you are engaged in at the moment. Do not let it wander to other subjects or to other places. If your body is in 57th Street, New York, do not have your mind in some other city.

If you are engaged in considering a certain subject, do not let your mind wander to other subjects; or else, if you must, stop thinking of the first subject and give your full attention to the other subject. In a few moments you will realize that this is not what you want to consider today, and you will return to the thing that matters and your thought is not likely to stray again.

The minds of many people are constantly dashing backwards and forwards in all directions. Naturally this makes poise impossible. Be quiet—not dull or necessarily silent, but quiet. You can be sociable and friendly and still be quiet mentally. All the mystics in all faiths, Eastern and Western, have taught this.

When you have acquired poise you will very, very rarely get excited, or angry, or frightened. You will not be gloomy. On the contrary, you will be happier than you have ever been before.

Practice poise in this way and you will be surprised how soon it will become a habit. Of course, you will not discuss this with other people. They will notice a change in you and their liking and respect for you will increase in a remarkable manner.

Be still, and know that I am God.

❧

Consecration

A SPECIFIC TREATMENT WILL SOLVE A PARTICULAR problem or a particular danger, and that is wonderful.

However, the most important thing in any one's life is that his general and habitual state of mind should be positive and spiritual. This will gradually change his whole consciousness and the conditions of his whole life. Also as time goes on it will give him great power in prayer, and therefore cause his specific treatments to succeed far sooner than would otherwise be the case.

In other words, it is not your state of mind, your outlook, and especially your feelings, as they exist from time to time, that matter much. It is your habitual and continuous convictions about God and about prayer that fundamentally govern your life.

That is to say, that if you want to make real and rapid progress and to bring harmony, peace and safety into your life, you must dedicate every phase of your life to the glory of God, and practice this policy. Naturally, this will be difficult at first, but if you mean business, it is only a question of time when you will find yourself doing it, not as an occasional thing, but as a habit— and this will be your real salvation. This is the true meaning of *consecration*. The consecrated life is the one in which you put God and His Will first, and it is the doorway to heaven here and now.

Note carefully that this kind of life certainly does not mean being solemn, much less gloomy. It does not mean retiring from the world, giving up innocent pleasures; and much less does it mean praying all day (which is not good). You should maintain your social contacts, live a normal Christian life in business, etc., but constantly remembering God, and avoid doing anything that you know would be displeasing to Him.

God wants us to be happy, joyous, and active—but always in His service.

Thou wilt keep him in perfect peace whose mind is stayed on Thee.

❧

Don't Be Selfish

YOU MUST NOT BE SELFISH IF YOU WISH TO HAVE any success in the spiritual life. In his Great Prayer, Jesus makes us say Our Father, and not simply my Father. We should draw the true lesson from this, and pray for others as well as for ourselves.

Some people take the mistaken view that we should not pray for ourselves at all but only for others, but this is to go to the opposite extreme. Pray every day (for a short time) for others as well as for yourself. This will have a much greater reaction than you will probably expect.

Pray for different groups of people at different times, as you feel led. Sometimes pray for sick people in hospitals who are likely to recover soon, and at other times pray for those who are spoken of as so-called "incurables." Of course, you will not admit to yourself that anyone is really incurable.

Sometimes pray for persons in jails, claiming peace, understanding, and freedom for them.

Sometimes pray for those who seem to have a special difficulty in finding suitable employment.

Sometimes pray for those who are lonely and feel themselves to be isolated.

From time to time God will inspire you with new groups to pray for, so that you will never feel that these ideas are getting stale.

Above all, pray for people who think that they do not believe in God or in prayer. Of course, they need your prayers more than anyone else.

All these prayers will bring back a special blessing to you yourself, besides blessing many, many people whom you will never even hear of.

"It is more blessed to give than to receive." Jesus Christ.

The Lord's Day

I AM OFTEN ASKED IF IT IS ESSENTIAL TO OBSERVE THE Lord's Day. In metaphysics, the answer is that we should make every day the Lord's Day. Whatever the name of the day may be we should remember that it belongs to God and that we should live it in that spirit. "This is the day which the Lord hath made; we will rejoice and be glad in it."

Of course, this does not mean that it is not good to have a day of rest once a week, for it certainly is; but nevertheless we should try to make every day in the week the Lord's Day.

Many people refer to Sunday as the Sabbath, but this is not the case. Sunday is properly called the Lord's Day because it has always been dedicated to the honor of Jesus Christ. The Sabbath is Saturday, which means the seventh day. Nevertheless, Saturday, the Sabbath is just as holy and sacred a day as any of the other six.

Let us dedicate every day to the service of God and seek to live in His Presence, and we shall have seven Lord's Days every week. This is what Jesus would have wished.

❧

The Remedy — Divine Love

IF WE HOLD NEGATIVE THOUGHTS, UNDER ANY PRE-text, those negative thoughts are being built into our consciousness. If we hold thoughts of hatred, criticism, or fear, we are building them into our consciousness; and what we build into our consciousness, expresses itself in our lives.

These negative things will appear in the body in the form of an ache, or a pain, or disease, or they may appear in business as anxiety or failure, or often they show up as inability to get along with other people.

Now there is one supreme remedy for this. We must fill our hearts with Divine Love, for Divine Love casts out all error.

Fill your heart with Divine Love and your body will begin to heal, your business affairs will begin to improve, people will feel more friendly to you and you to them, and above all, your fears and doubts will melt away.

How do you fill your heart with Divine Love? By realizing that the Love of God, Divine Love, is so great that it has compassion for everyone, that it sees the beauty and truth in every situation. You fill your heart with Divine Love when you seek to express these qualities in your everyday living.

Jesus said, *"By this shall all men know that ye are my* disciples, if ye have love one to another."

How Big Is God?

OLD-FASHIONED ORTHODOXY USED TO THINK OF GOD as a venerable sort of person, sitting off in the sky somewhere, meting out punishment or favors as He saw fit.

Savages in the jungle thought of God as a kind of great spirit dwelling perhaps in a lofty mountain. He was to be feared, and in order to gain His favor, He must be propitiated by various rites and incantations, often with human sacrifice.

Even in our own Old Testament, the peoples of those days felt that God demanded burnt offerings and other oblations; and they often ascribed to God some of their own shortcomings and failings.

In each of these cases, man, in his groping for the Truth, circumscribed and limited God, so that he only possessed a small fraction of the real God.

However, little by little over the centuries, man's concept of God has grown, until today, the student of metaphysics knows that God is not to be found in some remote place, but that He is immanent in His creation, and that means that He can be contacted right here and now.

How big is God? Your own concept of God can be big or small, but the bigger you build God, the greater influence will He be in your life. The more you see of God in yourself, your fellow man, and your environment, the more your life will reflect peace, poise, and joy.

Practice the presence of God in all things and you will find that not only will more and more good come into your own life, but you will become a source of inspiration and help to all those whom you meet.

❧

Give It the Right Thought

THERE ARE A NUMBER OF PHRASES USED MORE OR less commonly in metaphysics, sometimes without fully realizing their true import. Such a phrase is *give it the right thought*.

Now this expression is useful in handling a difficulty if we really understand what it means. It does not mean that having said, "I will give it the right thought," the matter is done with and nothing further is required. That is only "Pollyanna" or wishful thinking.

But we give a thing the right thought when we can say, "Thy Will be done," knowing that God's Will is always something good and glorious. We give a thing the right thought when we cast the burden on the Christ within. We give a thing the right thought when we pray about it, believing that God hears and answers prayer. We give a thing the right thought when we maintain a positive and affirmative attitude.

When we do these things we are relying on God instead of ourselves.

As a man thinketh in his heart, so is he.

Can Happiness Be Found?

VOLUMES HAVE BEEN WRITTEN ON THE SECRET OF happiness, but I like the simple old story that has been told so often.

In the old days, there was a king who was so miserable and unhappy that he called together all of his soothsayers, magicians, and other court advisers, to find a remedy. They tried all sorts of methods to rouse the king out of his deep despair—but alas, to no avail.

Finally, one of them suggested that a search be made for the happiest man in the kingdom, for it was thought that if the king could put on the man's undershirt, he would become happy too. In due course, the happiest man in the kingdom was found. But, of course, he had never even owned an undershirt. His happiness sprang from within.

This story well illustrates Jesus' instructions that we seek first the kingdom of God, and all other things will be added. Too often we do the reverse; we add all these other things and then try to find happiness.

But happiness is not something to be put on like an overcoat. It is to be found when we seek to put God first in our lives. For this it is that brings the joy that passeth all understanding—and the other things will be added too.

And ye shall seek Me, and find Me, when ye shall search for Me with all your heart (Jeremiah 29:13).

❦

Fasting

*This kind goeth not out but by prayer and
fasting.*   MATTHEW 17:21

THERE WAS A MAN WHO HAD AN EPILEPTIC SON, AND
Jesus' disciples had been unable to heal him. The
father in desperation appealed to Jesus and he promptly
healed the son. His disciples seeing this, inquired why
they had not been able to do the same. Jesus replied,
"Because of your unbelief. . . . This kind goeth not out
but by prayer and fasting."

Now, fasting from food is a good thing on occasion,
especially for those who have indulged in unwise habits
of eating. But Jesus could not have referred to physical
fasting, for at another time, he said, "It is not that
which goeth into the mouth that defileth a man; but
that which cometh out of the mouth." In other words,
it is not what we eat, but what we think in our hearts
and express, that is important.

It is your mental diet that determines the kind of life
you live. You must fast from thoughts of fear, anger,

94

resentment, condemnation, and so forth. It is these things that nullify your prayers. When you have thus cleansed your mind by this kind of fasting, you have begun to give all power to God—and, of course, your prayers will then be powerful too.

So long as you harbor thoughts of lack and limitation, your power in prayer will not be great, but when you fast from these negative things, then will your prayers be answered for yourself as well as for those for whom you pray.

No Mental Prop

Judge not according to the appearance, but judge righteous judgment.   JOHN 7:24

IT'S FUN TO WATCH A MAGICIAN PULL A RABBIT OUT OF an empty hat, or to see him produce a card or a coin seemingly out of the thin air. Were we to accept the evidence of our eyes as the truth, we would be persuaded to believe that he had really materialized these things. However, we judge not by the appearance, but rather

95

do we know that his art lies in quick and clever manipulation.

When driving along a country road, the hills and trees in the distance seem to move along with us, while the shubbery close by moves swiftly past us in the opposite direction. It would appear that the whole landscape was moving in one direction or another, and that possibly we were standing still. Of course, we know the truth of the situation, and judge rightly that it is only ourselves who are in motion.

However, in our spiritual lives we often accept the appearance for the reality.

For instance, we see sickness or lack, and, judging by the appearance, we come to the conclusion that these things are real. But the Bible tells us not to judge by appearance, but to judge righteous judgment. Now, what is righteous judgment? It is the judgment that comes from right thinking, and right thinking gives no power to anything but God, and therefore can produce nothing but good. So when we judge righteously we know that, as real as sickness and lack may seem, they are but the appearance and not the truth.

These negative things have no real substance except that which you give them by your mental support. So long as you accept them at their face value, they have become very real for you, and you must suffer with them until you have changed your mind concerning them.

So the first step in overcoming them is to *remove the mental prop* that you have given them by believing in them. As you steadfastly continue to judge not by appearance, but judge righteous judgment, you will find that, like the eagle which soars above the storm, you will be able to rise above the temporary conditions and frustrations of the material world—for God is the power and the glory.

The Power of the Word

The Bible says:

> *In the beginning was the Word, and the Word was with God, and the Word was God.*
> JOHN 1:1

ALWAYS ANTECEDENT TO THE WORD IS THE THOUGHT; and so here the Bible tells us that in the beginning was the thought and the thought was with God and the thought was God. The beginning does not refer to a date in history for God and His expression are infinite.

It means that the beginning of all expression is thought. In other words, there is a continual beginning with every thought we think. We are what we are because of the thoughts we habitually think, for these are the beginning of expression or manifestation in our lives. Therefore if we choose to think God-thoughts—positive, constructive, creative thoughts—we will express health, harmony, and prosperity in our lives.

> *He sent His word, and healed them, and de-*
> *livered them from their destructions.*
> PSALM 107-20

The preceding Verse 19 tells us that those who "cry unto the Lord"—those who pray—will be saved; and Verse 20 tells us why—because God always answers prayer. He sends His healing thought and thus delivers us from our destruction.

> *And they were astonished at his doctrine: for*
> *his word was with power.* LUKE 4:32

Of course, Jesus fully realized the power of the word. Again and again when someone came to him, he spoke the word of healing, and the person was immediately made whole.

> *So shall my word be that goeth forth out of*
> *my mouth: it shall not return unto me void,*

but it shall accomplish that which I please,
and it shall prosper in the thing whereto I
sent it. ISAIAH 55:11

You too have the power of the word. Not only is your thought powerful in bringing healing to your body, but it will also produce harmonious and prosperous conditions in your life, because your surroundings are the outpicturing of your thoughts.

For the word of God is quick, and powerful,
and sharper than any two-edged sword.

If . . .

IF YOU ARE NOT HELPING THE OTHER FELLOW, YOU are not helping yourself.

If you choose the lower when you see the higher, you are not giving all power to God.

If you say one thing, and do another, you are not living up to the highest you know.

If you are minding somebody else's business, you cannot be minding your own.

If you fill your mind with resentment, criticism, and anger, you will reap that reward.

If you have no sense of humor, the joy of the Lord is not your strength.

If you want to be on the spiritual path, you must practice the Presence of God at all times.

Take a Vacation — From Yourself!

DURING THE SUMMER WHEN VACATIONS ARE IN order, it is a good time to take a vacation from yourself. Of course, you cannot leave your body at home and go off somewhere, but nevertheless, you can change your mind and your habits of living so that for practical purposes you will be having a vacation from yourself.

Here are a few simple suggestions:

1. Change your habits of thought. Be sure to eliminate all resentment, criticism, and condemnation of

yourself as well as others, no matter how plausible the pretext for harboring them.

2. Change your habits of eating. Include some new articles of food that you have not been in the habit of eating—and drop some of the old ones.

3. Keep your prayers fresh, new and simple. Get away from the usual phrases and affirmations.

4. Rearrange, if possible, your order of work at the office or shop. Resolve any old grievances.

5. Reorganize your recreation and leisure. Add some new pastime and eliminate some of the old ones. Try reading a different newspaper, and get acquainted with other magazines than those to which you are accustomed.

6. Drop all cares and worries about politics, business, and the foreign situation. You will be surprised to find that the world will manage to struggle on somehow.

Take a vacation from yourself—and you might like the change well enough to make it permanent.

Preparing for Peace

P AUL SAYS THAT FAITH WITHOUT WORKS IS DEAD. In other words, one should not sit and pray only, but he should also take the necessary material steps. It needs a combination of the two things to bring success.

It may be, in our personal lives, that taking the necessary material steps may mean going to an employment agency to look for a job, or getting a medical examination, or seeking legal advice. In each case, having prayed first, we know that God is directing our footsteps along the right paths. Sometimes we put the cart before the horse by taking the material steps first, and then saying in effect, "Look God, what I have done. Please confirm my actions," or, "Please get me out of this mess."

So, as a nation, the necessary material steps may mean building a strong economy, stock-piling essential materials, co-ordinating the efforts of labor, management, and government, and the hundreds of other things that will make a country strong.

But through it all, we should prepare for peace by constantly praying for peace, because only in that way will the material steps that we take have any real meaning in the long run.

The world needs a spiritual revival, and in praying for peace for this nation and its friends, we should also pray for our potential enemies as well. Hate is the essence of war—love is the essence of peace. See the Christ in all men.

Blessed is the nation whose God is the Lord (Psalm 33:12).

✿

An Ounce of Prevention

THE OLD ADAGE, "AN OUNCE OF PREVENTION IS worth a pound of cure," is just as true in the spiritual life as it is in the material world.

A great many people wait to make their contact with God until a serious difficulty is upon them and then they hasten to find a spiritual solution. Of course, it is better to seek God under such circumstances than never to find Him at all, because God is ever ready and willing to help us when we turn to Him in prayer.

But why wait for trouble? There is many a difficulty that could be prevented or lightened if we were to make our contact with God now, and put our lives on the Spiritual Basis.

The Bible does not say to wait until some future time to find God. It says *now* is the day of salvation. *Now* is the accepted time.

If you will put your life in God's hands now through daily prayer and meditation and a complete willingness to do His Will, you will find that your problems will grow less as time goes on, and you will have acquired that serenity and poise that only God can give. Then, come what may, nothing shall disturb you.

And now, Lord, what wait I for? My hope is in Thee (Psalm 39:7).

Spotlights

TO SPEND TIME IN NEGATIVE THINKING IS MERELY
to add disappointment to disappointment.

It is not the chosen who are saved, but those who choose God.

To recognize the ideal is the first step in bringing it forth in our lives.

Live one day at a time. To worry over tomorrow's demands is to lose sight of today's blessings.

Rid your mind of the negative things so that there may be room for the positive.

There are a thousand good starters for one good finisher.

To trust in God with one part of your mind and harbor fear in the other part, is to be a house divided against itself.

Happy is he that hath the God of Jacob for his help, whose hope is in the Lord his God (Psalm 146:5).

Reunion

A GREAT MANY OF OUR PROBLEMS ARISE FROM OUR separation from God in thought or deed. Sometimes that separation comes about unconsciously when our affairs seem to be going well and for the moment we forget God. Sometimes the separation is deliberate when we see the higher and choose the lower. Sometimes the separation is due to a lack of true understanding of God and His nature.

In the first two cases it is easy to see and understand the cause of the separation, and the obvious remedy for our reconciliation or reunion with God.

However, it is not always so simple a matter to comprehend that we can separate ourselves from God through a lack of true understanding of His nature.

Jesus, it will be remembered, constantly made a point of his at-one-ness with God, saying again and again that it was not himself that did the works but the Father in him. So to begin with, we separate ourselves from God when we pray to Him afar off, as it were, instead of realizing that God dwells in us and we in Him.

We also separate ourselves from God when we believe that prayerful repetition will make God "change His mind" in our favor. God is unchanging Principle and manifests in accordance with Divine Law. We bring about our reunion with Him when we realize that our good already exists in Divine Mind, and that we have but to remind ourselves through prayer of this fact, to bring that good into manifestation. We never have to convince God of our need, but rather do we have to convince ourselves that God has already provided for our good.

Meditate on these things in order to bring about that perfect union with God which will make you powerful in prayer and demonstration.

※

The Company You Keep

WHAT KIND OF COMPANY DO YOU KEEP? Do you like the kind of people you normally associate with? There is an old adage that says that a person is judged by the company he keeps.

If you find that you would like to make some changes in the company you keep, there is not much use in the long run to look around and make some new selections. You will first have to make a change in the kind of company you keep in your mind.

When we continually harbor thoughts of anger, fear, resentment, jealousy, criticism, and so forth, we eventually bring these things into manifestation in one form or another.

That means that you will find that you will have surrounded yourself with people who reflect your state of mind.

If you want to improve the kind of company you keep, see to it that you are keeping mental company with love, joy, peace, and harmony, and above all, that you are constantly seeing the Christ in the other fellow.

You will be surprised to find that the people you meet will be living up to the new standard you have set in yourself.

Whatsoever a man soweth, that shall he also reap (Galatians 6:7).

❧

The Health of My Countenance

Why art thou cast down, O my soul? and why art thou disquieted within me? hope thou in God: for I shall yet praise Him, who is the health of my countenance, and my God.

PSALM 42:11

THIS SHORT VERSE IS REALLY A COMPLETE SERMON in itself for it points the way out of a state of nervousness and depression to a healthy condition of mind, body, and affairs—the real joy of living.

In this verse, the psalmist pauses to ask himself, "Why am I cast down? Why do I shake with nervousness and fear? Why is my very soul disquieted within me?"

And as he reflects upon these things, the answer comes to him—as sooner or later it must to all of us—trust in God! And he determines that in spite of appearances, he will continue to praise Him who is the health of his countenance.

The word "countenance" stands for the power of recognition, and "health," in this case, stands not only for bodily well-being but also for the "health" of all our affairs.

In other words, when we recognize God as the source of all good, and are willing to trust in Him, we begin to manifest a healthy condition in our bodies and in our external affairs. Nervousness and fear evaporate and we once again have a sense of true well-being.

There is another important point, and that is that we should always praise God for His Name's sake—He who is my God—without any thought of profit or reward. This is true contemplation.

❧

Tales of Woe

THE NEGATIVE THINGS IN LIFE OFTEN ARE THE ONES that get the most attention from the public. Thousands of couples live harmonious married lives, but one divorce can get a two column spread in the newspapers. A man leaves his fortune for the care of the aged and he might be favored with a line or two on the inside pages; but a racketeer can have his picture on the front page.

At first glance it might seem peculiar that we should consider that such negative things are news, but on closer examination it easily appears that this is so because mankind really believes that good is the normal thing and to be expected, and that therefore the opposite is news.

Now, our chief mistake is not in recognizing man's deviation from good as news, but in constantly filling our minds with these happenings. And there are many people who are not content with merely reading an account of an unhappy event, but can hardly wait to recount the dreadful details to any who will listen.

Of course, this kind of conduct can only bring inharmony and unhappiness in its wake.

If you want to demonstrate peace of mind, harmony, friendship, and prosperity, see to it that you channel your thought along positive and constructive lines. Concentrate on the good that is to be found everywhere. Soon the negative things will drop out of your own life, and the world too will look a lot better to you.

Read Philippians 4:8.

✠

Awaken the Christ

*And they awake him, and say unto him,
Master, carest thou not that we perish?*

MARK 4:38

JESUS AND HIS DISCIPLES HAD GONE INTO A BOAT TO cross a lake. As so often happens on lakes and small bodies of water, a storm came up suddenly. His disciples were filled with fear and apprehension because the wind was so great that the boat was rapidly filling with water—but Jesus was asleep!

The disciples' first thought was to awaken the Master (the Christ) for they felt that here was a situation that had gotten beyond them. He arose and said unto the sea, "Peace, be still," and the storm subsided. Then he turned to his disciples and asked them, "Where is your faith that you are so fearful?"

Now the Christ is asleep in each one of us until we become aware that God is not to be found afar off but dwells within us.

When the storms (the problems) of life assail you, and it appears that your ship is about to founder, then it is high time that you awaken the Christ within you. Recall to mind that God in you is able to cope with any difficulty, to bring peace and harmony in any situation. Then will the Christ whisper to you, "Peace, be still. Let your fearful trembling cease."

The biblical account goes on to say that not only did the storm abate but there was a great calm. This is exactly what happens when we have awakened the Christ within. We have turned our burden over to God. The storm subsides, and a great calm comes over us—the peace that passeth all understanding.

Spring Cleaning

SPRING IS THE SEASON FOR THE TRADITIONAL SPRING cleaning. It is a time for the removal of the winter's accumulation of dust, and dirt, and debris. It is a time for making all things new.

Nature herself furnishes a tremendous inspiration for

this activity. What has looked bare and brown since fall, suddenly bursts forth in a newness of scent and color. Winter's desolation is over. All the world has awakened.

Now, there is an esoteric significance to spring. Man has felt intuitively that there is a springtime of the soul —a time when the winter of limitation and separation is over, a time when the soul awakens to the Presence of God.

Too often, however, we have allowed a "winter's" accumulation of old negative thoughts and beliefs so to fill our souls that a thorough job of spring cleaning is necessary.

So let this springtime be the season for the removal of old prejudices, petty deceits and jealousies, false vanities, and the hundred and one little negative things that many of us hang on to so fondly.

Let a new day dawn! Open the windows of your soul to the light of God's inspiration and understanding. Let the fresh air of God's love revivify you, and thrill you.

Awaken to the glory that is within for only then will you truly find the glory that is in the outer!

And I saw a new heaven and a new earth (Revelation 21:1).

Up Till Now

IT IS SOMETIMES SAID: "WHAT IS THE USE OF TREAT-
ment? Up till now my treatments have produced
very little result." The answer to this is that in very
many cases treatment has produced extraordinary and
dramatic results. "It has subdued kingdoms, wrought
righteousness, obtained promises, stopped the mouths
of lions, quenched the violence of fire, turned the edge
of the sword, out of weakness made strength, and
turned to flight the armies of hell," not only in Bible
times, but in our own age and day.

If it is objected that one treatment or one week of
treatment does not make the complete and final demonstration, that, apparently, one will be required to go on
praying all his life, this is perfectly true. We are required to go on praying all our lives. But it may be
added that as we progress in the quality of our prayers,
they will not be a burden, but a joy and a refreshment—
and in any case, there is no other way.

It is also said, and it is perfectly true, that in some

cases there is very little result to show for treatment; but this only means either that the patient or his healer has not been treating in the right way (and this is to be remedied by praying for guidance); or that the difficulty is very deeply seated in consciousness and is requiring more treatment than has yet been given.

Because one does not yet see a result it does not at all follow that no work has been done. But in any case, the remedy is still—more treatment, because, there is simply not any other way out of trouble.

The Lord also will be a refuge for the oppressed, a refuge in times of trouble (Psalm 9:9).

❦

Our Daily Bread

DIVINE METAPHYSICS TEACHES THAT SCIENTIFIC Prayer, or the Practice of the Presence of God, will, sooner or later, bring health, prosperity, and harmony into our lives.

In fact, more often than not, it is with the direct and immediate object of obtaining one of these things that people take up the study at all. It is often said that the vast majority come into Truth because they are "down and out" in one of these respects, and this is probably correct.

There is no objection to coming into Truth in this way. Indeed, it is inevitable that it should often be so. Our difficulties arise from using our free will in opposition to the Will of God, and we do not abandon that abuse of power until we have realized that there is no good to be found in that direction.

As long as we come to God for any reason, it is well. The only thing that matters is that we do seek the Kingdom of God and His Righteousness, and, provided we have done that, we should not waste any time in the analysis of motive. That is merely plowing the sand.

The important thing is that, having come into Truth for whatever reason, you should remind yourself again that the Christ Truth teaches that though we live on a physical plane which is full of poverty, struggle, sin, sickness, and death, these things nevertheless can be destroyed by persistent daily prayer.

Give us this day our daily bread (Matthew 6:11).

✻

Be Practical

NOT SO VERY MANY YEARS AGO, TO SPEAK OF A PRAC-
tical religion would have been considered irreli-
gious if not actually sinful by the majority of Christians.
Religion was something one found at church on Sunday, and was to be put on along with one's Sunday
clothes.

Even today there are many people who feel that religion is something entirely separate and apart from their
daily lives. Indeed, there are many who believe that,
instead of being a practical matter here and now, the
fruits of religion are really to be found in the next world!

Yet the curious anomaly is that Jesus himself was the
most practical teacher that ever lived. There was nothing
vague or theoretical about his teaching. To him, religion
was everybody's daily life. As he went about speaking
to the multitudes he not only sought to make his teaching practical to them, but he demonstrated in his own
life how practical religion could be. His many healings

of the sick and his overcoming of all kinds of difficulties, bear eloquent testimony of the views of Jesus on the practicality of religion.

Now, there are two ways in which we can make our religion practical.

We must first make it practical in our own lives, by using the principles Jesus taught, to demonstrate over problems as they come along, and to elevate our consciousness so that our lives may be an example to others. This is really a lifetime job in itself, but it will bring increasing harmony, happiness, and prosperity.

The second step is to make your religion practical for others by making it possible for them to get a better knowledge of the Truth. This can be done by the distribution of metaphysical booklets and books, or by suggesting where one might find the same instruction that has helped you.

You should also make your religion practical for others by praying for them when they request it, and by giving material help where this seems genuinely indicated.

Of course, you will find that in doing these things you have, as the Bible says, let your own light so shine that you have become an example and an inspiration to those whom you meet.

Cast Anchor!

THERE ARE MANY CHANGES GOING ON IN THE WORLD today and, in general, this is a good thing. Without change there could be no progress. Of course, not all change in itself is good, but when things are changing it means that sooner or later, good will emerge from the cross currents of ideas and policies which change brings about.

Now, if events seem to be changing too rapidly for you to cope with, remember that there is one thing that never changes, and that is Spirit or God. God is the eternal, loving Father Who is always ready to say, "Fear not, child, for all is thine." As the old hymn so simply puts it:

> *The storm may roar without me,*
> *My heart may low be laid;*
> *But God is round about me,*
> *And can I be dismayed?*

When your ship is being tossed about by the storms of change, remember that God is your Anchor. No matter what the outer world may be doing, your inner world can be peaceful and calm because God is never failing in His Power and Love.

For I am the Lord, I change not (Malachi 3:6).

❧

What Does God Expect?

AS CHILDREN OF THE MOST HIGH WE HAVE A DIVINE heritage and therefore a right to expect that God will take care of us in every way. We should expect him to heal us when we are sick, to furnish us with abundance when we are in need, and to bring us peace and harmony when we are filled with fear.

The Bible is full of promises as to what God will do for His children, but perhaps Jesus put it the most plainly when he said, "What man is there of you, whom if his son ask bread, will he give him a stone, or if he ask a fish, will he give him a serpent? If ye then, being evil, know how to give good gifts unto your children, how much more shall your Father which is in heaven give good things to them that ask Him?"

So you have a divine right to expect all these good things from God.

But what does God expect of us? Well, God has a right to expect that we will put Him first in our hearts. That means that we will see God in all things and in all persons—in short, the Practice of the Presence of God.

Then God expects us to have a lively faith. To the extent that we lack faith, we deny God. Faith in itself is a reliance upon the goodness of God.

And lastly, God expects us to go to Him in prayer—not as a miserable suppliant, but as a son of God who knows that even before he has asked, the loving Father has answered.

Spiritual Résumé

PRAYER IS THE CORNERSTONE UPON WHICH THE Truth teaching rests because it is man's direct contact with God. From time to time, it behooves us to review the principles that make our prayers powerful.

1. *Pray daily*. In prayer, as in other human activities,

practice makes perfect. Praying daily brings increased ability to pray successfully.

2. *Pray simply.* If your prayers are becoming literary masterpieces, to that extent they are lacking in power. Jesus told us to approach God with the simplicity of a little child.

3. *Pray gently.* In prayer, effort defeats itself. Remember that you are communing with God and He does not have to be forced into a decision.

4. *Pray with faith.* Believe that the prayer that you are now making is the one that is being answered. Jesus told us to believe that we have received and we shall receive.

5. *Affirm your good.* You do not have to beg God to do something. He has already provided for your good. It is your privilege, through prayer, to bring that good into your consciousness.

6. *Give thanks.* Giving thanks for the good you expect from your prayer is really another indication of your faith in God and prayer. If there is a high road to demonstration, it is through praise and thanksgiving. Jesus terminates the magnificent "Lord's Prayer" with praise to God—"For *Thine* is the Kingdom, and the Power, and the Glory."